CONFUSING CREATURE NAMES

HEDGEHOGS ARE NOT HOGS!

By Lincoln James

Gareth Stevens
PUBLISHING

Please visit our website, www.garethstevens.com. For a free color catalog of all our high-quality books, call toll free 1-800-542-2595 or fax 1-877-542-2596.

Library of Congress Cataloging-in-Publication Data

James, Lincoln.
Hedgehogs are not hogs! / by Lincoln James.
p. cm. — (Confusing creature names)
Includes index.
ISBN 978-1-4824-0952-9 (pbk.)
ISBN 978-1-4824-0953-6 (6-pack)
ISBN 978-1-4824-0951-2 (library binding)
1. Hedgehogs — Juvenile literature. I. James, Lincoln. II. Title.
QL737.E753 J36 2015
599.33—d23

Published in 2015 by
Gareth Stevens Publishing
111 East 14th Street, Suite 349
New York, NY 10003

Copyright © 2015 Gareth Stevens Publishing

Designer: Michael J. Flynn
Editor: Greg Roza

Photo credits: Cover, p. 1 ValentÃn RodrÃguez/age fotostock/Getty Images; pp. 5, 11 Mr. Suttipon Yakham/Shutterstock.com; p. 7 (shrew, hedgehog) Erni/Shutterstock.com; p. 7 (mole) Santiu/Shutterstock.com; p. 9 (European hedgehog) Kichigin/Shutterstock.com; p. 9 (long-eared hedgehog) Kefca/Shutterstock.com; p. 9 (four-toed hedgehog) Zhukov Oleg/Shutterstock.com; p. 13 (main) Lena Lir/Shutterstock.com; p. 13 (quills) Marcel Derweduwen/Shutterstock.com; p. 15 Tomas Hilger/Shutterstock.com; p. 17 wentus/Shutterstock.com; p. 19 Otto & Irmgard Hahn/Picture Press/Getty Images; p. 21 KAMONRAT/Shutterstock.com.

Printed in the United States of America

CPSIA compliance information: Batch #CS15GS: For further information contact Gareth Stevens, New York, New York at 1-800-542-2595.

CONTENTS

Boldface words appear in the glossary.

What Is That?

Hedgehogs love searching hedges and bushes for tasty bugs, worms, and small animals. While doing this, they make a **grunting** noise, somewhat like a pig. That's how they got their name! If hedgehogs aren't hogs, what are they?

Hedgehogs Are Mammals

Like pigs and hogs, hedgehogs are **mammals**. Other mammals include dogs, horses, whales, and people. Hedgehogs are very different from most other mammals. The hedgehog's closest **relatives** are shrews and moles.

hedgehog

mole

shrew

7

Around the World

There are about 15 kinds of hedgehogs. They're originally from Europe, Asia, and Africa. However, people have taken them all over the world. In places with cold, snowy winters, some hedgehogs sleep all season long.

European hedgehog

long-eared hedgehog

four-toed hedgehog

9

Looking Good!

Hedgehogs are small animals. Depending on the kind, they can weigh between 7 ounces and 2.2 pounds (200 and 1,000 g). They have small, black eyes and pointy **snouts**. Their fur and **quills** can be brown, gray, white, or black.

Hedgehog Quills

Of course, a hedgehog's most noticeable feature is its quills. A hedgehog has about 6,000 quills. Quills help keep it safe. When there's trouble, the hedgehog rolls up into a small, **spiky** ball. Few predators can eat such a pointy animal!

quills

13

Predators

Some animals eat hedgehogs, but not many. Some of their most feared predators are large birds, such as owls. An owl's long claws and sharp beak are perfect for getting past hedgehog quills. Other predators include dogs, wolves, foxes, and weasels.

15

What's for Dinner?

Hedgehogs love to eat tiny critters they find under bushes, such as bugs, worms, and snails. They will eat larger animals, too, such as snakes and frogs. Hedgehogs also eat roots, mushrooms, bird eggs, and fruits. They even eat bees and wasps!

Growing Up

Mother hedgehogs have around three to seven babies at a time. Babies can't hear or see at first. They grow soft quills that fall out within a few days. Stronger quills grow in, but they fall out, too. Then, even stronger quills grow in.

19

Pet Hedgehogs

Hedgehogs are often kept as pets, but they aren't like most pets. They're often shy around people, but they can be quite friendly once they get used to you. The hardest part about owning a hedgehog is picking it up without getting hurt!

Caring for Hedgehogs

Find out if your town and state allow you to keep hedgehogs as pets.

Hedgehogs need a lot of water.

Hedgehogs will eat many things, but not everything is good for them. They like to eat bugs, meat, and some kinds of fruit.

Hedgehogs love playing and hiding. Make sure they have plenty of toys and places to hide.

Make sure the cage is big enough. Some owners allow their hedgehogs to run free.

GLOSSARY

grunt: a low noise made by an animal

mammal: a warm-blooded animal that has a backbone and hair, breathes air, and feeds milk to its young

quill: a long, sharp body part that is somewhat like fur

relative: one of two or more animals that have many of the same features

snout: an animal's nose and mouth

spiky: having many sharp points, or spikes

FOR MORE INFORMATION

BOOKS

Doudna, Kelly. *Hilarious Hedgehogs*. Minneapolis, MN: ABDO, 2013.

Leach, Michael. *Hedgehog*. New York, NY: PowerKids Press, 2009.

WEBSITES

Hedgehog
a-z-animals.com/animals/hedgehog/
Read more about hedgehogs and see pictures of them.

Hedgies.com
www.hedgies.com
Learn more about hedgehogs and how to take care of them as pets.

INDEX